Steven

Spielberg

Groundbreaking Director

Essential Lives

STEVEN
SPIELBERG
GROUNDBREAKING DIRECTOR

by Sue Vander Hook

Content Consultant:
Andrew Gordon, PhD
Professor of English, University of Florida

ABDO
Publishing Company

CREDITS

Published by ABDO Group, 8000 West 78th Street, Edina, Minnesota 55439. Copyright © 2010 by Abdo Consulting Group, Inc. International copyrights reserved in all countries. No part of this book may be reproduced in any form without written permission from the publisher. The Essential Library™ is a trademark and logo of ABDO Publishing Company.

Printed in the United States.

Editor: Holly Saari
Copy Editor: Paula Lewis
Interior Design and Production: Becky Daum
Cover Design: Becky Daum

Library of Congress Cataloging-in-Publication Data
Vander Hook, Sue, 1949-
  Steven Spielberg : groundbreaking director / by Sue Vander Hook.
     p. cm.—(Essential lives)
  Includes bibliographical references and index.
  ISBN 978-1-60453-704-8
  1. Spielberg, Steven, 1946—Juvenile literature. 2. Motion picture producers and directors—United States—Biography—Juvenile literature. I. Title.

  PN1998.3.S65V36 2010
  791.4302'33'092--dc22
  [B]
                              2008055527

TABLE OF CONTENTS

In 1994, Steven Spielberg won his first Oscar for Best Director for his film
Schindler's List. The film also was awarded the Oscar for Best Picture.

An Oscar at Last

On March 21, 1994, the sixty-sixth
Academy Awards were held in Los
Angeles, California. Some of the most famous
actors, directors, writers, and musicians filled the
four-tiered, 3,197-seat Dorothy Chandler Pavilion.

Throughout the huge hall, names of the greatest films of 1993 resounded—*Schindler's List*, *The Piano*, *Jurassic Park*, *The Fugitive*, *Philadelphia*. Awards were given for the "best" in every category—best picture, best actor, best actress, and more.

One film, *Schindler's List*, dominated the evening. As expected, the widely praised, agonizing drama about the Holocaust won Best Picture. But would its director, Steven Spielberg, walk away with the Oscar for best director? The award had eluded him for 16 years. Spielberg, widely considered the most successful director in Hollywood, had been nominated for the award three times previously. But the Academy had passed him by for directing *Close Encounters of the Third Kind*, *Raiders of the Lost Ark*, and *E.T. the Extra-Terrestrial*—all box-office favorites.

Toward the end of the more than three-hour ceremony, actor and director Clint Eastwood stood alone at the podium and read the nominees for Best Director: Jim Sheridan for *In the Name of the Father*, Jane Campion for *The Piano*, James Ivory for *The Remains of the Day*, Steven Spielberg for *Schindler's List*, and Robert Altman for *Short Cuts*. Eastwood opened the envelope and announced, "The Oscar goes to, big surprise, Steven Spielberg."[1]

The crowd exploded with applause and rose to their feet. Spielberg kissed his wife, Kate Capshaw, and made his way to the platform. Visibly shaken, he briefly embraced Eastwood and clutched the Oscar statuette with both hands. "Whoa, Whoa," he uttered softly into the microphone as he nervously brushed his forehead with his hand. "I have friends who have won this before." The audience laughed, and Spielberg continued,

But, and I swear, I have never held one

The Oscars

The first Academy Awards ceremony took place on May 16, 1929, in Hollywood, California, to honor the best in film for 1927 and 1928. The hosts were actor Douglas Fairbanks and director William C. DeMille. More than 250 people attended the meal and 15-minute presentations that followed. In 1944, the Academy Awards were aired on radio, followed by black-and-white televised coverage in 1953 and color in 1966.

Commonly called the Oscars, the Academy Awards are presented every year by the Academy of Motion Picture Arts and Sciences (AMPAS) to honor professionals in the film industry. Winners in each category receive a gold-plated statuette informally called an "Oscar." Although the origin of the nickname is not clear, there is a story that the statuette reminded the Academy's librarian of her Uncle Oscar, and the name stuck with the staff. In 1934, the press called it an Oscar in a newspaper column. The Academy eventually adopted the name. The statuette features a knight gripping a sword with both hands and standing on a reel of film with five spokes. Each spoke stands for the original award categories: actors, directors, producers, writers, and technicians. Today nearly 6,000 members of AMPAS vote annually for the best in up to 25 categories of filmmaking.

before. This is the first time I've ever had one of these in my hand. Wow. Oh dear. Let me just start by saying that this never could have happened—this never could have gotten started—without a survivor named Poldek Pfefferberg who Oskar Schindler saved from Auschwitz, from Belsen. He's the man who talked Thomas Keneally into writing the book. I owe him such a debt; all of us owe him such a debt. He has carried the story of Oskar Schindler to all of us, a man of complete obscurity who makes us wish and hope for Oskar Schindlers in all of our lives.[2]

Based on a True Story

Spielberg continued to thank those who had made *Schindler's List* a success. And then, choking back tears, he added, "And to the 6 million who can't be watching this, among the one billion watching this telecast tonight, thank you."[3] The 6 million referred to the Jews

Holocaust Tragedy

The Holocaust (*Shoah* in Hebrew) refers to the genocide of European Jews during World War II (1939–1945). Adolf Hitler, dictator of Nazi Germany, wanted to kill all Jewish people in the world, a plan he called the "Final Solution of the Jewish Question." In 1944, Hitler increased his killing of Jews, transporting hundreds of thousands by train and truck to concentration camps. From May to July, more than 500,000 Hungarian Jews were transported to the Auschwitz-Birkenau concentration camp in Poland. When they arrived, many of them were killed with poisonous gas. In total, nearly 4 million Jews were killed at seven concentration camps, which accounted for more than half of the 6 million Jews killed in the Holocaust.

Spielberg directing Liam Neeson on the set of Schindler's List

who had lost their lives in concentration camps during World War II. These people were the story of *Schindler's List* and the reason Spielberg made the movie. Some of them were his relatives, family members from Poland.

Some Jews, such as Poldek Pfefferberg, had survived the atrocities and passed on their stories. Pfefferberg had immigrated to the United States three years after the war. In 1980, he told his remarkable story to a customer who bought a briefcase at his leather-goods shop. The customer was novelist Thomas Keneally. Pfefferberg (now called Leopold Page) told Keneally that he had the "best story of the century" for him. He told him about Oskar Schindler, the Nazi who hired him and his wife to work in his factory. Their jobs saved them from being transported to concentration camps where Nazis were exterminating Jews and other "undesirables." In fact, Schindler had become an unlikely hero to more than 1,100 Jews who worked in his enamelware and ammunitions factories in Poland and Czechoslovakia.

Keneally was interested in what Pfefferberg had to say. He traveled to several countries to talk to nearly 50 of "Schindler's Jews," as they were called. In 1982, *Schindler's Ark* by Thomas Keneally was published. It would take ten years and hundreds of phone calls before Pfefferberg would convince Steven Spielberg to make the novel into a movie.

In 1992, Spielberg finally agreed to make *Schindler's List*. Pfefferberg accompanied Spielberg to Poland to show him the factory where he had worked, the Jewish ghetto, and the

"To the right, many of the barracks have been torn down, but the chimneys are still there. It's a forest of chimneys. It was a city. It was an industry, an industry of death. It is a haunted killing field, and you feel it. Everybody was extremely edgy the couple of days we shot there."[4]

—*Steven Spielberg in 1993, describing the Auschwitz-Birkenau concentration camp that was filmed for* Schindler's List

concentration camps. For his entire life, Spielberg had been ashamed of being a Jew. Filming *Schindler's List* forced him to travel down the dark path of his past. Now for the first time, he could accept who he really was. "I was hit in the face with my personal life," he admitted. "My upbringing. My Jewishness. The stories my grandparents told me about the *Shoah* [Holocaust]. And Jewish life came pouring back into my heart."[5]

Schindler's List was Spielberg's triumph that night at the Oscars, and Pfefferberg and his wife were there to share it with him. But it was not Spielberg's only accomplishment. *Jurassic Park*, his science-fiction tale about cloned dinosaurs in the modern world, won three Oscars—Best Sound, Best Sound Effects, and Best Visual Effects. By the end of the evening, Spielberg's films won ten Oscars—seven for *Schindler's List* and three for *Jurassic Park*. It was a well-earned achievement for the 47-year-old director who had passionately been making films since he was a child. ⌒

Spielberg may be the most recognizable Hollywood director.

Steven with his father and mother in 1947

GROWING UP JEWISH

teven Allan Spielberg was born on
December 18, 1946, at the Jewish Hospital
in Cincinnati, Ohio. He was one of more than
3 million babies born that year in the United States.
It was the beginning of what came to be called the

baby boom. World War II had ended the year before, and millions of soldiers streamed home to resume life and start their families. Arnold Spielberg, an enlisted army radioman, was no exception.

STEVEN'S PARENTS

Arnold and Leah had married a few months before the war ended. After Arnold's discharge from the U.S. Army, the newlyweds settled into a comfortable apartment in Avondale, a largely Jewish neighborhood in Cincinnati. Like millions of other veterans, Arnold enrolled in college under the new GI Bill of Rights. He would eventually graduate from the University of Cincinnati with a degree in electronic engineering and pursue a successful career in the growing field of computers. Leah had already graduated from the university with a degree in home economics, but her real passion was music. She had studied at the Cincinnati Conservatory of Music and was a talented pianist. While pregnant with Steven, Leah spent hours each day playing classical music. After Steven was born, she held him on her lap while she practiced. Steven would later say, "If I weren't a filmmaker I'd probably be in music. I'd play piano or I'd compose."[1]

From Memory to Movie

Steven Spielberg's first memory was of darkness followed by a bright, sudden light when doors were opened to the Adath Israel synagogue in Cincinnati. His parents later told him he was around six months old at the time. At one end of the synagogue, a bright red light illuminated the Ark of the Torah. Above, there was a domed skylight with a chandelier that hung from a Star of David. As an adult, Spielberg used parts of that memory in *Close Encounters of the Third Kind* when a three-year-old boy stands in the doorway of his house and stares at the blinding orange light of an unidentified flying object (UFO).

Leah also brought creativity and fun to the Spielberg household, which suited Steven's curious nature. He later remarked, "We never grew up at home, because *she* never grew up."[2] It was a Peter Pan atmosphere, fueled by Leah's nightly readings of the story. Steven admitted later that he had always felt like the boy from Neverland. "It has been very hard for me to grow up," he confessed. "I'm a victim of the Peter Pan Syndrome."[3] But with this characteristic came a powerful imagination and the freedom to boldly see the world as a fantasy, with an added touch of science fiction.

Steven's father stood in contrast to Leah. Although Arnold was fascinated with science fiction, he looked at the world logically. He hoped his son would share his scientific interests and encouraged him to study math and science. But Steven was not interested in those subjects.

ESCAPING HIS JEWISHNESS

In 1952, the Spielbergs moved just outside Camden, New Jersey, to Haddon Township, a suburban area with a mixture of mostly non-Jewish, middle-class families. It was the first time the Spielbergs had not been surrounded by people who shared their faith, and they often felt out of place. Steven complained about being different, especially at Christmastime when their neighbors adorned their houses with bright lights, Santas, and nativity scenes. Begging

Arnold Spielberg

Steven Spielberg's father, Arnold Spielberg, enlisted in the U.S. Army in January 1942. He served first in Karachi, Pakistan, as a shipping clerk, and then as a ham radio operator with a B-25 bomber squadron. Arnold was in charge of the communications room, first in Pakistan and then near Calcutta, India. World War II was already well under way when he enlisted. It had begun in September 1939 when Germany invaded Poland. Arnold's squadron was nicknamed "The Burma Bridge Busters" for their skill at destroying Japanese communications and railways.

In December 1944, Arnold returned to the United States, to Dayton, Ohio, where he served until Japan surrendered on August 15, 1945. Arnold and his new bride, Leah, settled in Cincinnati, Ohio, one of the oldest Jewish communities in the Midwest. Arnold's father, Shmuel Spielberg, had emigrated there from Russia in 1906. Two years later, in 1908, Shmuel brought Rebecca Chechik to America; they were married that year. Not all of the Spielbergs came to the United States. Some relatives eventually became victims of the Holocaust during World War II in Poland and Ukraine. Arnold estimated that 16 to 20 of his relatives died at the hands of the Nazis in the first half of the 1940s.

his father to decorate their house was hopeless. Steven's parents would not conform to their neighbors' traditions. Even though they did not attend synagogue very often, the elder Spielbergs still held firmly to their Jewish heritage.

As long as Steven could remember, his parents and grandparents had talked about their roots and their relatives who died in World War II because they were Jewish. Steven's grandmother taught English classes to German Jewish immigrants. Many of them had survived the concentration camps and found postwar refuge in the United States. Steven listened to their stories of extreme fear and undeserved mutilation during "The Great Murder," or Shoah, the Hebrew word for the Holocaust. But his Jewishness was not something Steven wanted to think about. It only reminded him of how different he felt.

Religious Instruction

Three days a week after school, Steven went to the Hebrew school at Temple Beth Shalom in Haddon Township, New Jersey, for religious training. Rabbi Albert Lewis remembered Steven as a very quiet child who did what he was required to do. Steven was a member of the temple's Cub Scout troop, but the rabbi felt Steven still needed to learn to express himself and develop social skills.

WORLD OF WONDER

Steven preferred a world of adventure and imagination, filled with endless things to explore. Friends and neighbors described him as energetic, smart, and curious. While Steven was curious, he was also fearful of many things. He was terrified of the maple tree that swayed in the breeze outside his bedroom window. The streetlight behind the tree cast haunting shadows on his wall at night. Steven's vivid imagination saw grotesque monsters with twisted heads and countless arms. He was afraid of almost everything—cracks in the wall and monsters under his bed. One of Steven's greatest fears was the dark. To Steven, those nighttime hours held a world of unknown creatures and strange events. Television and movies scared him, including *Dragnet*, the death of Bambi's mother, and the wicked queen in *Snow White and the Seven Dwarfs*. But despite those fears, he was still fascinated with movies and television. Although his father restricted how many movies and television shows he could watch, Steven still managed to see plenty of both as he was growing up.

Steven often coped with his fears by scaring or bullying others. "I began telling stories to my younger sisters," he admitted. "This removed the fear from my soul and transferred it right into theirs."[4] One time he locked them in the closet where he had hung a skeleton with a light glowing in one eye socket. Another time he served his youngest sister, Nancy, a plate of lettuce and tomatoes with the head of her favorite doll in the center.

Steven lived in a world of wonder mixed with fear. He carried most of his fears with him to Edison School in Haddonfield, where he walked around in a daydream and kept to himself. School did not interest him, and he usually got Cs, which disappointed his mother. When Steven was 11, the Spielbergs moved to Arizona. It was around this time that he found something to capture both his imagination and fears in a constructive way.

The Greatest Show on Earth

The first movie Steven Spielberg ever saw was *The Greatest Show on Earth*. It was directed and narrated by Cecil B. DeMille, one of the most famous film directors of the first half of the twentieth century. The film won the 1952 Oscar for Best Picture. It starred Charlton Heston as the circus manager and James Stewart as a strange clown who never takes off his makeup, even when the show was over. Spielberg would one day meet Heston at Universal Studios and invite him to lunch.

A scene from The Greatest Show on Earth, *the first movie Steven saw*

Steven was hooked on filmmaking from the moment his father loaned him the family camera.

Boy with a Camera

rnold Spielberg had been filming amateur home movies since the early 1930s when the first Kodak 8 mm camera came out. But Steven constantly criticized his father's films and said he could do better. Tired of his son's negative comments, Arnold finally handed the camera over to Steven, who became the family filmmaker. He filmed everything—his family at home or at a campsite, his neighbors and schoolmates, and even the hubcaps of the family car as it pulled out of the driveway.

Steven took the camera wherever he went. It was a fanatical hobby, but it was also his protection from the world. "I don't mind looking the world in the eye," Steven once said, "as long as there's a movie camera between us."[1] Safely behind his camera, Steven's insecurity turned into boldness. He could hide his face, the face that continually embarrassed him with its protruding nose and ears. He could block out the bullying and the religious slurs directed at him. He momentarily forgot that he was an awkward skinny kid with acne who did not have a lot of friends. His camera also protected him from his

"Fear is a very real thing for me. One of the best ways to cope with it is to turn it around and put it out to others. I mean, if you are afraid of the dark, you put the audience in a dark theater."[2]
    —*Steven Spielberg on using his camera to overcome his fears*

worst fears—even while he filmed scenes that vividly depicted those fears, whether real or imaginary. But most of all, behind the camera, his "actors" listened to him. His sister Anne recalled,

> *If you looked at a picture of him then, you'd say, "Yes, there's a nerd. There's the crew cut, the flattop, there are the ears. There's the skinny body." But he really had an incredible personality. He could make people do things.*[3]

A Growing Talent

At age 11, Steven's filmmaking talent earned him an Eagle Scout merit badge. When he was not able to come up with an idea to earn the highest rank in the Boy Scouts, his father suggested that he film a Western in the desert. Steven took his advice and made what was called *The Last Gunfight*. The movie made his fellow Scouts clap, cheer, and laugh. And the film earned Steven his merit badge. But it did more than that. Steven later said,

> *[It gave me] a sense of power bossing around a few kids who otherwise would be slapping me around. But that wasn't so important. I was making something happen that I could relive over and over again, something that would only be a memory without a camera in my hand.*[4]

Steven's movies became so popular in the neighborhood and at school that kids started asking to be part of his cast. Anne said, "He made everything he was going to do sound like you wished you were a part of it."[5] The family's living room turned into a movie studio. Bright lights shone on Steven's actors—his sisters, his mother, neighborhood kids, and anyone else he could find. Steven's mom sewed costumes and cooked up cherries that doubled as blood for special effects. She drove the cast into the desert when Steven needed to film on location.

No one could quite figure out the secret of Steven's camera work. He

Boy Scouts

Steven Spielberg received his Eagle Scout merit badge when he was 11. The rank of Eagle Scout is the highest rank in the Boy Scouts of America. To earn the rank, a Scout must exhibit leadership, service, and outdoor skills. A Scout must also earn merit badges that are awarded when a Scout masters a certain skill.

The skill Spielberg mastered was filmmaking. His film was a Western, shot at a restaurant where a red stagecoach was parked out front. With cap guns and bandannas over their noses, Steven's fellow Scouts and other friends robbed the stagecoach while two people sat on the driver's bench. The camera shots did not show the front of the stagecoach, so no one knew there were no horses attached. In a scene where one of the characters was hurled over a cliff, Steven used a dummy made of pillows dressed in clothes and shoes. Ketchup doubled as blood on the rocks. Steven's fellow Scouts loved his film, and Spielberg's confidence grew. After that, he took his camera with him on every scouting trip.

would climb up on the wing or nose of a wartime fighter plane parked at the airport and shoot scenes that looked like the plane was climbing, banking, or diving. He set up a backdrop in his yard that resembled the cockpit of a fighter plane; he used a household fan for the wind. Then he combined his authentic-looking footage with real footage of World War II dogfights. The result was a movie that amazed its viewers.

Finding His Niche

In September 1961, Steven began his freshman year at Arcadia High School in Phoenix, Arizona. Still very short and thin, Steven got shoved around a lot by some students at his school. Throughout his high school years, he was the kid who was made fun of in the locker room and pummeled by his fellow students outside the shopping center. But despite the humiliation, he learned to go about his independent way. Steven played the clarinet in the band and joined the drama department. Connecting with students who enjoyed theater arts made him realize "there were options besides being a jock or a wimp."[6]

But most of Steven's time was consumed with filmmaking. He knew what he wanted to do—make movies—and he did that as often as possible. School was not important to him, and he often pretended to be sick so he could stay home and edit his films.

Steven was 15 years old when he finished his 40-minute film *Escape to Nowhere*. For two years, he had worked on this action-packed World War II saga. It featured a mostly teenage cast, realistic special effects, and wartime props, including a machine gun. Steven's mother had a part in it, too. She donned a helmet and played a German soldier. A local television crew showed up during the filming. Reporter Barry Sollenberger recalled,

> He had a pickup truck with a 50-caliber machine gun mounted in the back. I remember how awed we were: "Man, where does this guy come up with this 50-caliber machine gun?" But I had enough foresight to say, "The machine

An Early War Movie

When Steven Spielberg filmed *Fighter Squad,* a 15-minute, black-and-white World War II movie, he persuaded the workers at the Phoenix airport to let him use a real World War II B-51 bomber that was parked there. One of his friends played the part of the pilot, donning Arnold Spielberg's goggles and flight jacket as his costume. Steven climbed up on the plane, taking a close-up of the "pilot" who had an evil grin on his face. Then Steven got a close-up of the pilot's thumb as it pushed a button. Then he cut to real footage of a warplane with blazing guns. Footage of *Fighter Squad* and *Escape to Nowhere,* another short war film, were later featured in a 1999 special edition DVD of Spielberg's Academy Award-winning film, *Saving Private Ryan.*

gun—heck, where does a [teenager] come up with a pickup truck?"[7]

The police also showed up, and Steven's dad had to convince them that they were shooting a movie and doing nothing else.

At the 1962–63 Canyon Films Junior Film Festival, *Escape to Nowhere* won first prize. Steven won a 16 mm Kodak movie camera. But since 16 mm film was so expensive, Steven and his father traded the camera in for an 8 mm with a zoom lens, stop motion, and slow motion. Arnold also purchased a projector and sound system that made it possible for Steven to record sound onto the film.

At the end of his sophomore year of high school, Steven finished writing a 67-page screenplay for his next movie, *Firelight*. The script was about a group of scientists investigating mysterious colorful lights in the sky and the subsequent abduction of animals and people. The cast was made up of high school students and family members.

8 mm Film

Steven Spielberg liked using an 8 mm movie camera, the kind his father first let him use. Eastman Kodak first developed the film, which is 8 millimeters wide, during the Great Depression of the early 1930s. The intent was to provide something less expensive than the wider 16 mm film, which was first introduced in 1923. A typical spool of 8 mm film could capture from three to four-and-a-half minutes of action.

Spielberg used better equipment as he progressed in filmmaking.

Steven's four-year-old sister, Nancy, was the star—the little girl abducted by the alien firelight. Steven composed the music for the soundtrack. First he played it on his clarinet, and then his mother transposed it to the piano and finally to a written score. The Arcadia High School band performed the music, which Steven recorded and added to the film. *Firelight* took six months to film.

In 1964, *Firelight* was finished and ready for a private preview. The cast and crew gathered in the

Spielbergs' living room and watched in amazement the science-fiction thriller that their friend, brother, and son had created. Steven would one day say about that day: "I knew what I wanted, and it wasn't what my dad wanted for me: I wanted Hollywood."[8]

For the film's premiere showing, Steven's father rented the Phoenix Little Theatre, and Steven sold tickets for a dollar each. On March 24, the 2-hour-and-15-minute film dazzled 500 viewers with its realistic action, color, and sound. The local Phoenix newspaper wrote that Steven could expect great things to come. The movie made a profit of $100.

The next day, the Spielbergs moved to Saratoga, California. Arnold Spielberg had accepted a job with IBM in northern California's Silicon Valley. It was a huge step up in his computer career. Although Steven was not happy about moving again, California would provide him with the opportunity he needed to enter the world of filmmaking and become a successful director.

Lost Film

When Steven first looked for work in Los Angeles, he submitted two reels of his film *Firelight* to a producer. Steven wanted to show him his filmmaking talent. A week later the company went out of business, but the producer never returned Steven's reels. Only portions of *Firelight* still exist today.

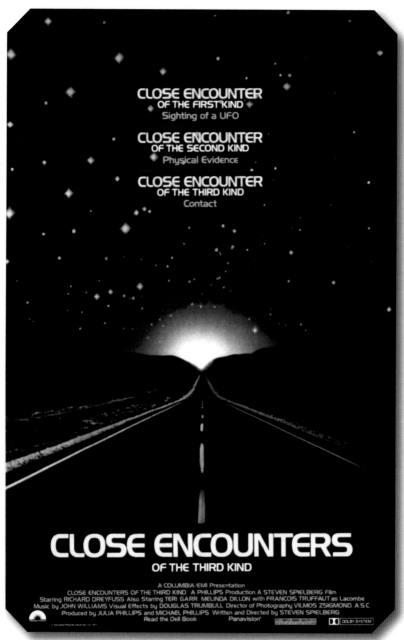

A still from Spielberg's 1977 film, Close Encounters of the Third Kind, *which stemmed from* Firelight

After the Spielbergs moved to California, Steven interned at Universal Studios.

A Foot in the Door

The Spielbergs arrived in California in March 1964. Their first home was in Los Gatos, a classy suburb of San Jose. On the edge of Silicon Valley, the city was the high-tech center of the United States. Arnold jumped wholeheartedly into his new job designing a computer for IBM, and Steven enrolled in the local high school for the last two-and-a-half months of his junior year. When school was out in June, the Spielbergs moved again, this time to Saratoga, another upscale neighborhood about 50 miles (80.5 km) outside San Francisco. In September, Steven began his senior year at Saratoga High School, which he later described as "hell on earth" and the worst experience of his life.

Tough Time in California

Affluent Saratoga High School was not the kind of place a nerdy kid could blend in. And being Jewish gave some kids even more reason to bully Steven. "I got smacked and kicked to the ground during P.E., in the locker room, in the showers," he remembered.

> *People coughed the word "Jew" in their hand as they passed me in the hallway. We couldn't stop it. So my mom picked me up in her car every day after school and took me home.[1]*

Steven covered up his anger and countered the bullying with humor and sarcasm, and then he would walk away. He evened the score with the athletes by filming their games and writing about them in *The*

Falcon, the school newspaper. He always included
a fair dose of criticism, a tactic that sometimes
backfired and fueled more harassment.

Steven's troubles were not limited to school,
however. At home, his mother and father were not
getting along, and Steven and his sisters felt the
tension. He later said,

> *My sisters and I would stay up at night, listening to our parents*
> *argue, hiding from that word [divorce]. And when it traveled*
> *into our room, absolute abject panic set in. My sisters would*
> *burst into tears, and we would all hold one another.* [2]

Universal Studios

Steven had visited Universal Studios when he was
about 16 years old. A friend of his father had set up
a private tour for Steven with Chuck Silvers, head
of Universal's editorial department. The friend
described Steven as a "film bug" and asked Silvers to
show him around. Silvers said,

> *That first conversation [with Spielberg] was a mind-blower*
> *for me. Steven was such a delight. That energy! . . . At some*
> *point in time, it dawned on me that I was talking to somebody*
> *who had a burning ambition, and not only that, he was going*
> *to accomplish his mission.* [3]

During the summers of 1964 and 1965, Steven worked as an unpaid apprentice at Universal Studios. He worked for Silvers, doing clerical work and running errands. Steven also wandered around the lot, gazing at movies and television shows being filmed and dreaming of directing his own. He watched movie icon Alfred Hitchcock, "the master of suspense," direct his movie thriller *Torn Curtain*. Steven also talked to whomever would give him a minute of time.

Universal Studios

Located in Universal City, California, Universal Studios is the second-oldest motion picture company in the country. In 1909, a German Jewish immigrant named Carl Laemmle started the company, originally called the Yankee Film Company, with Abe and Julius Stern. Yankee soon became the Independent Moving Picture Company. In 1912, it combined with eight smaller companies to create the Universal Film Manufacturing Company. It would eventually be called Universal Pictures Company, Inc.

In 1915, Laemmle built Universal City Studios, the world's largest motion picture complex located near Hollywood on 230 acres (93 ha). By the late 1950s, the rise of television had shut down Universal, and the company sold its then 360 acre (146 ha) studio lot to the Music Corporation of America (MCA) for $11 million. In 1962, MCA took over Universal Pictures, which became an active movie studio with some of the top actors and directors. Universal's focus then turned to television. For a time, Universal provided nearly half of all prime-time shows for NBC and introduced the made-for-television movie. Spielberg's hits, including *Jaws*, *E.T. the Extra-Terrestrial*, and *Jurassic Park*, restored Universal's place in the movie industry and helped secure its financial stability.

Steven had graduated from Saratoga High
School in 1965 with low to average grades. After
graduation, he moved in with his father, who rented
an apartment in Los Angeles.

COLLEGE AND A CAREER

In 1965, the United States sent marines into
Vietnam. It was also the year Steven had to register
for the draft. The law required that all 18-year-old
males register with the Selective Service System. This
motivated Steven to attend college and possibly avoid
being drafted and sent to Vietnam.
He also had a burning desire to be a
filmmaker and wanted to attend one
of the best filmmaking schools in the
country. He applied to the University
of Southern California (USC) and
the University of California, Los
Angeles (UCLA), but his grades were
not good enough. Even attempts by
Chuck Silvers of Universal Studios
to pull rank at USC were not enough
to get Steven into the cinema
department. But that did not stop
Steven, who started figuring out a way

Steven's Parents Divorce

Steven's mother and
father separated after
his high school gradu-
ation. In 1966, they
finalized their divorce.
Leah moved back to
Phoenix with her daugh-
ters, 16-year-old Anne,
12-year-old Susan, and
9-year-old Nancy.

to break into the film industry on his own.

In the fall of 1965, Steven enrolled at California State University, Long Beach. The college did not have a film department, so he majored in English. It was not what he wanted, but it kept him out of Vietnam and gave him something to do while he figured out how to break into the movie industry. Most importantly, the school was less than an hour from Universal Studios. Steven drove back and forth from his apartment to college and, as often as possible, to Universal Studios. He scheduled his college classes on two days of the week so he would have

at least three days a week at Universal, hoping to convince someone to give him the break he needed. But most people in the film industry did not take him seriously. They were not interested in his 8 mm films and told him he would have to film with 16 mm or 35 mm film in order for anyone to watch the outcome.

While working at Universal Studios, Steven met with several famous actors, including Rock Hudson, left, and Cary Grant, right.

Steven's solution to the problem was a part-time job in the college cafeteria, which earned him enough money to rent a 16 mm camera and purchase wider film. Essentially ignoring his schoolwork, Steven spent his time working, filming, and roaming around Universal Studios. He invited actors to lunch, and some of them—Charlton Heston, Cary Grant, and Rock Hudson—accepted his invitation. He hung out with Sonny and Cher, the popular singing-comedy duo. He got to know some of the biggest directors of the time, such as Francis Ford Coppola and John Cassavetes. Steven also visited with the film editors, watching what they were doing and constantly asking questions.

In 1967, Steven started filming his first 35 mm film about high-speed bicycle racers in the desert. He called it *Slipstream*. But Steven never finished the film. On the last weekend before the borrowed and rented equipment had to be returned, the sky dumped torrential rains where the last scene was going to be shot.

The unfinished project discouraged 20-year-old Steven, but it did not defeat him. In July 1968, he began filming *Amblin'*, a 26-minute, 35 mm film with no dialogue. It told the simple story of a hippie boy and girl in the late 1960s who hitchhike from the desert to the California coast. This became Steven's entrance into the world of film. It would also be his ticket to professional filmmaking and his assurance of a job at Universal

Filming *Amblin'*

The success of *Amblin'* landed Steven a contract with Universal and made him the youngest director to ever get a long-term contract with a major Hollywood studio. The filming of *Amblin'* began in July 1968 in a studio. But then the unpaid crew went on location, first to a beach house in Malibu and then to several California desert locations. Because of the unbearable desert heat, many members of the crew walked off before the shoot was over. *Amblin'* won several awards as well as a showing at the 1969 Atlanta Film Festival.

Sid Sheinberg

Sid Sheinberg began working for MCA/Universal Studios in 1959. In 1973, the 38-year-old entertainment manager became president of the huge movie and TV studio. Under his leadership, Universal Pictures produced the three highest-grossing films over three decades: *Jaws* in 1975, *E.T. the Extra-Terrestrial* in 1982, and *Jurassic Park* in 1993. The three films were all directed by the director whom Sheinberg is credited with discovering—Steven Spielberg. In 1990, Sheinberg was honored with an Honorary Life Membership in the Directors Guild of America.

Studios. Chuck Silvers cried when he saw *Amblin'*. Silvers said, "It was everything it should have been. It was perfect." He also said,

> *Steven Spielberg is as close to a natural-born cameraman as anybody I've ever known of. . . . As far as I'm concerned he's the most gifted person in motion pictures. Not just today—ever.* [4]

Once Silvers figured out what to do with the talented filmmaker, he called Sidney Sheinberg, the president of Universal TV. A week later, Steven had a seven-year contract with Universal Studios. His salary was $275 a week, and his job was directing television shows and possibly movies made for TV. Steven's dream was coming true. And now, despite what his father might think, he quit college, not bothering to go back and even clean out his locker. Directing was what he had always wanted to do. Now he plunged headlong into the world of professional filmmaking.

At age 21, Steven Spielberg landed a seven-year directing contract with Universal Studios.

*Steven Spielberg directing Joan Crawford in "Eyes,"
his first television segment*

WORLD OF FILM

On December 18, 1968—Steven Spielberg's twenty-second birthday—*Amblin'* premiered at Loew's Crest Theater in west Los Angeles. Although the *Los Angeles Times* called *Amblin'* a "splendid film," it took a backseat to Otto

Preminger's *Skidoo*, a short film about hippies and free love. But Spielberg had already moved beyond *Amblin'*. In November 1969, his first television segment of "Eyes" aired on NBC's *Night Gallery*, a series of paranormal tales.

Over the next five years, Spielberg directed TV series such as *Marcus Welby, M.D.* and *Columbo*. But directing television shows became just a job for him. He yearned to direct movies to satisfy his desire to create. He later recalled that he was uncertain if he wanted to continue directing. "I didn't have that passion, because television sort of smothered the passion," Spielberg reflected.[1]

In 1971, this changed. Universal bought film rights for "Duel," a short story about a driver stalked by a trucker on a lonely desert road. When Spielberg convinced the studio to let him direct *Duel*, he eagerly began shooting the 74-minute TV movie and recaptured his passion.

Big Debut

On Saturday night, November 13, 1971, *Duel* aired on television as ABC's Movie of the Weekend. The instant hit catapulted Spielberg into the world of film and secured his reputation as a first-rate director. Famous directors such as David Lean (*The Bridge on the River Kwai* and *Lawrence of Arabia*) praised him as a bright new director. *Duel* was released in Europe and won the grand prize at the Festival de Cinema Fantastique in France. It also took the award for best first film at the Taormina Film Festival in Italy.

Spielberg wanted to break away from television, but he was still under contract with Universal Studios for another four years. He tried to satisfy his hunger for filmmaking with movies made for TV. In January 1973, Spielberg began filming *Sugarland Express* in San Antonio, Texas. The movie fulfilled Spielberg's directing desire for a while and received rave reviews. But the reviews did not affect the public, who largely rejected the movie and doomed it to commercial failure. When Spielberg heard the disappointing news about *Sugarland*, he was already filming

Sugarland Express

The film *Sugarland Express* was based on the true 1969 account of Ila Fae Dent, who helped her husband, Robert, escape from a Texas prison. As the couple fled, they kidnapped Texas state trooper Kenneth Crone and held him hostage in their car. They were pursued by approximately 150 police cars as well as cars and helicopters filled with reporters. Robert was killed by an FBI agent and a county sheriff. Ila Fae served five months in prison. The movie was filmed on location at the Beauford H. Jester prison facility.

Spielberg, center right, *with cast members on the set of* Jaws

another movie, one that would surely have audience appeal. He ignored his failure in *Sugarland Express* and focused on what would be the greatest success of that time—*Jaws.*

PROBLEMS WITH *JAWS*

Spielberg had begged to direct *Jaws* and vowed to make the horror movie about a great white shark a box-office blockbuster. But he had to overcome many problems before this would happen. Filming took three times longer than the schedule allowed, and production costs doubled and then tripled. There were so many problems that the crew started calling it *Flaws* instead of *Jaws*. Spielberg often wanted to resign and direct another film. But Sid Sheinberg would not let him quit. Sheinberg said, "I literally forced him to do it. . . . I think he was upset for a while. He turned to me and said, 'Why are you making me do this B movie?'"[2]

When filming began in May 1974, few cast members had been hired. And there was no script because Spielberg had rejected two screenplays. He hired screenwriter Carl Gottlieb to

Storyboards

A storyboard is a series of drawings, created either by hand or digitally on a computer, that illustrate the sequence of events in a film. It is a visualization of what should be seen through the camera lens once shooting begins. Storyboard scenes are often sketched on separate pieces of paper and taped or tacked to a wall. Some are crude drawings with stick figures sketched by the director; others are created with elaborate detail by a professional artist. Still other storyboards are digitized or computer-generated drawings. A film's storyboard helps the camera crew and the cast know what the director is visualizing for each scene. Some directors, such as Steven Spielberg and Alfred Hitchcock, have relied heavily on storyboards.

Storyboarding began at Walt Disney Studio in 1933 with *The Three Little Pigs,* an animated cartoon. The first live action film to use storyboards was *Gone with the Wind,* the 1939 film that won ten Academy Awards. Production designer William Cameron Menzies was hired to draw every shot of the film. Storyboarding eventually became a valuable tool in business and industry as a way to design and plan processes, projects, ad campaigns, and Web sites.

help him write enough of the script each night to get by during the next day's filming. When they ran out of script, the actors improvised.

The ocean and the weather caused a different set of problems. The weather changed from day to day, making it hard to match shots. One day the ocean was calm and glassy, and the next day it might be choppy. But Spielberg insisted on filming *Jaws* in the ocean rather than in a water tank in a studio. He wanted the shots to be as realistic as possible.

The biggest problem, however, were the three mechanical sharks. Saltwater negatively affected the automated creatures and often hindered their functioning. When a shark was working, Spielberg madly gathered actors and extras together to capture some shark footage. He also filmed gruesome attack scenes without a shark. It turned out to be a clever strategy, implying that the

Real Shark Footage

Off the coast of Australia in 1975, Ron and Valerie Taylor were filming real shark footage to be used in *Jaws*. A dwarf actor was hired to be lowered into the water in a miniature shark cage—all to make the great white shark look enormous. The plot called for the man in the cage to be killed by the shark, but before the scene could be shot, one of the sharks got trapped in part of the empty cage and destroyed it. Only a few shots of the violent scene were used in the film.

shark was there, hidden just beneath the surface. The combination of suspense and ominous music stirred up fear that derived from the unknown.

PERSEVERANCE PAYS OFF

Spielberg proved to be a master of menace with *Jaws*. He transferred his fear of water and of the unknown to the audience. It was what he had done to his sisters time and again—he removed the fear from his soul and transferred it right into theirs. At the preview of *Jaws* in New York, his sister Anne said, "For years he just scared us. Now he gets to scare the masses."[3]

Jaws was released in June 1975, taking in more than $100 million and breaking all previous box-office records. The 28-year-old Steven Spielberg had created the most profitable film in motion-picture history up to that time. The public went wild over *Jaws*; the press called it "Jawsmania." *Jaws* won Academy Awards for Film Editing, Sound, and Original Music Score. The Academy did not nominate Spielberg for Best Director, however. His film was not serious enough for them. But it appealed to the masses, and it appealed to Spielberg. He was filming what audiences wanted to see.

Jaws *broke previous box-office records and became Spielberg's first blockbuster.*

ALIENS AND A NEW IDEA

After *Jaws*, Spielberg began working on a science-fiction film, *Close Encounters of the Third Kind*. The film was about an electrician who encounters strange events and becomes obsessed with finding out what is behind them. Spielberg wrote the script for *Close*

Encounters of the Third Kind, a takeoff on
Firelight, the film he had debuted when
he was 17. The script intertwined
his childhood fantasies, his real-life
experiences, and his fascination with
science fiction.

Unlike the gruesome alien movies
that Spielberg watched as a child, *Close
Encounters of the Third Kind* highlighted
the friendly nature of aliens—the
contact and the connection—not the
conflict. Although Spielberg evoked
a foreboding feeling from simple
objects in the movie such as a child's
toy or a household appliance, he also
creatively transformed that fear into a
childlike wonder.

Whenever Spielberg has directed
a movie, he has been a perfectionist,
demanding the best from his cast and
crew. He has constantly come up with
new ideas, expanding the original
ideas and scope of the film. Producer
Michael Phillips recalled,

Types of Close Encounters

In Spielberg's science-fiction thriller, *Close Encounters of the Third Kind,* an encounter of the first kind is a sighting of an alien. The second kind of encounter is when a person has physical proof that aliens exist. An encounter of the third kind is when a human makes contact with an alien.

We had six wrap parties on Close Encounters. *We popped the champagne six times. Each time we thought we were finished, he would come up with a great idea that warranted going out and picking up something else. Steven always comes up with new ideas that make the movie better.*[4]

Close Encounters of the Third Kind, which opened in November 1977, was an instant hit. *Time* magazine praised the film's childlike point of view and overall direction. "Spielberg's reputation is no accident," the *Time* writer declared. "His new movie is richer and more ambitious than *Jaws*, and it reaches the viewer at a far more profound level than *Star Wars* [directed by George Lucas]."[5]

Close Encounters of the Third Kind propelled Spielberg's career to another level. It also raised the bar for future movies and directors. The film that grossed $270 million at the box office was also nominated for nine Academy Awards. It won two Oscars: Best Cinematography and the Special Achievement Award for sound effects editing. Spielberg received his first nomination for Best Director but did not win. He admitted that an Oscar was not his ultimate goal. Entertaining the audience was more important to Spielberg than winning an award.

Before *Close Encounters of the Third Kind* was finished, Spielberg's creative mind was already developing another idea for an action film in the style of James Bond. Spielberg talked with his friend and fellow director George Lucas about the idea. The two filmmakers brainstormed about a film they could do together. Lucas told Spielberg that he had a great character—one better than James Bond. Several years later, their character would take root in Indiana Jones and *Raiders of the Lost Ark*.

Music

John Williams's first original score for a Spielberg film was *Sugarland Express*. Williams has created the music for every professional film that Spielberg has directed except *The Color Purple* and *Twilight Zone: The Movie*. Williams has been nominated for 45 Academy Awards, the second-most nominations that an individual has received (Walt Disney received the most). He has won five Oscars: *Fiddler on the Roof* (1971), *Jaws* (1975), *Star Wars* (1977), *E.T. the Extra-Terrestrial* (1982), and *Schindler's List* (1993). Williams has also composed the scores for epic films such as *Superman*, *The Towering Inferno*, and the *Harry Potter* series.

Close friends George Lucas, left, and Steven Spielberg, right, have worked together on numerous films, including the four Indiana Jones movies.

Spielberg studying a model of the Raiders of the Lost Ark *set*

FILMS AND FAMILY

*D*uring the casting of *Close Encounters of the Third Kind*, Steven Spielberg had met actress Amy Irving. She auditioned for the female lead in the film, but Spielberg told her right away that she was too young for the part. A short time later, Irving landed a major role in the horror movie *Carrie*. Spielberg and Irving began seeing each other, and their relationship grew. Before long, Irving moved in with Spielberg in his home near Laurel Canyon. A few months later, they moved to a huge, five-year-old house in Coldwater Canyon near Beverly Hills. They called it "the house that *Jaws* built" because it was purchased with the money Spielberg made from *Jaws*. The film had made him a multimillionaire.

Indiana Jones

Around this time, Spielberg again focused on an idea that he and George Lucas had talked about earlier in their careers. Spielberg and Lucas brainstormed to create the saga of an archaeology professor-turned-swashbuckler who risks his life to recover a golden idol from an ancient temple. Both men had been fascinated as children with old 1930s and 1940s action-adventure series. Now they were going to create their own twist on the tales. Although neither Spielberg nor Lucas wrote the script, they concocted scenes such as the opening where Indiana Jones escapes certain death as he outruns a giant boulder.

While *Raiders of the Lost Ark* was developing,
Spielberg and Irving split up. They had been
together for four years and engaged for three
months. Spielberg was devastated by the breakup.
It was the most upsetting event in his life since his
parents' divorce. But he admitted that it helped
him grow up emotionally. "I've spent so many years
hiding from pain and fear behind a camera," he
said. "I avoided all the growing-up pains by being
too busy making movies. I lost myself to the world
of film. So right now, in my early thirties, I'm
experiencing delayed adolescence."[1]

Raiders of the Lost Ark, released on June 12, 1981,
became an instant hit and rose to the top in the
history of film with a gross of $363 million. It
received stellar reviews, including praise from
Vincent Canby of the *New York Times,* who called it
"one of the most deliriously funny, ingenious and
stylish American adventure movies ever made."[2] The
film was nominated for eight Academy Awards and
won four: Best Sound, Best Film Editing, Best Visual
Effects, and Best Art Direction-Set Direction. It also
earned the Special Achievement Award for Sound
Effects Editing. Spielberg was nominated for Best
Director—but again he did not win.

Spielberg directing Harrison Ford, who played Indiana Jones

RETURNING TO WONDER

Despite *Raiders of the Lost Ark*'s runaway success, Spielberg was disappointed in himself. "While I was doing *Raiders*," he said, "I felt I was losing touch with the reason I became a moviemaker—to make stories about people and relationships."[3] He longed to return to his childhood sense of wonder. In a 1982 interview, Spielberg explained how this led to his next movie idea:

While working on Raiders, I had the germ of an idea. I was very lonely, and I remember thinking I had nobody to talk to. . . . I began concocting this imaginary creature. . . . Then I thought, what if I were ten years old again—where I've sort of been for thirty-four years, anyway—and what if he needed me as much as I needed him? Wouldn't that be a great love story? So I put together this story of boy meets creature, boy loses creature, creature saves boy, boy saves creature— with the hope that they will somehow always be together, that their friendship isn't limited by nautical miles.[4]

And thus, *E.T. the Extra-Terrestrial* was born.

Spielberg drew from his childhood experiences when

Behind the Scenes of E.T.

E.T. was a new directing experience for Spielberg in two main ways. *E.T.* was the first film on which Spielberg worked mainly with child actors—Henry Thomas (Elliot), Robert MacNaughton (Michael), Drew Barrymore (Gertie), and the numerous children who helped E.T. get home. It was also the first movie he directed without using storyboards. The director who always planned ahead and was so prepared left much of the action to the spontaneous instincts of the children.

Carlo Rambaldi, who created the aliens for *Close Encounters of the Third Kind*, also designed the lovable alien in *E.T. the Extra-Terrestrial*. He said E.T.'s face was inspired by the faces of Carl Sandburg, Ernest Hemingway, and Albert Einstein. Four heads of E.T. were made for the movie, one for movement and the others for various facial expressions. An E.T. costume was worn at various times by one of two dwarfs or a 12-year-old boy who was born without legs. E.T. cost $1.5 million to create. Spielberg said it was "something that only a mother could love."[5]

he created Elliot, the boy who coaxed E.T. out of hiding and helped the friendly, frightened alien. *E.T.* was Spielberg's personal story—his parents' divorce, his loneliness, and his failed attempts to fit in with mainstream kids. E.T. was the friend he had always longed for. "When I was a kid," he said, "I used to imagine strange creatures lurking outside my bedroom window, and I'd wish that they'd come into my life and magically change it."[6]

E.T.'s success was extraordinary. At its premiere at the 1982 Cannes Film Festival, the audience was on their feet, stomping, shouting, and cheering their approval before the last scene ended. A huge searchlight scanned the auditorium until it found Steven Spielberg in the front row of the balcony, standing with a silly grin on his face. He called the experience "very humbling." A steady stream of moviegoers flooded theaters for an entire year before Universal Studios pulled *E.T.* from the market. Spielberg's share of the profits amounted to approximately half a million dollars per day.

Indiana Jones: Part Two

In 1984, Spielberg collaborated again with George Lucas, this time to make *Indiana Jones and the Temple of Doom*, a dark, grisly counterpart to *Raiders of the Lost Ark*. Many people at the screening were appalled, and critics claimed that Spielberg and Lucas violated the audience's trust by making a film that did not fit into the category of family entertainment.

Harrison Ford again played the part of Indiana Jones, or "Indy," as he was called. Spielberg cast Kate Capshaw for the role of Indy's girlfriend. During the filming, there was a spark of friendship between Spielberg and Capshaw, but at about the same time, Amy Irving came back into Spielberg's life. She surprised him at an airport in India, where he was scouting locations for the *Temple of Doom*. The two fell in love again.

The next two years were jam-packed for Spielberg. In 1984, Spielberg cofounded Amblin Entertainment. The company's logo was a silhouette of E.T. riding

E.T.'s Bad Review

Not all reviews of *E.T.* were positive. George F. Will wrote in *Newsweek*, "Well, I Don't Love You, E.T."[7] He claimed that the movie spread "subversive" ideas about childhood and science.

in Elliot's bicycle basket and flying in front of the moon. Amblin had a $3.5 million office complex, paid for by Universal Studios. The complex featured a screening room with a popcorn and candy counter, two cutting rooms, a video arcade, a kitchen run by a professional chef, a gym, gardens, an outdoor spa, and a wishing well with a miniature *Jaws* shark.

In 1984 and 1985, Spielberg produced *Gremlins*, *The Goonies*, *Back to the Future*, and *Young Sherlock Holmes*. He also directed *The Color Purple*, the story of a young African-American girl who endures abuse, poverty, and racism. Spielberg was in the middle of directing a scene for the film when Irving called with news that she was in labor. The next day, June 13, 1985, Irving gave birth to the couple's son. Spielberg called the baby his "biggest and best production of the year."[8] They named their son Max

The Color Purple

The Color Purple was adapted from a book of the same name by Alice Walker. In 1983, the book received the Pulitzer Prize for Fiction and the National Book Award. Before Walker would allow Spielberg to direct the film, she interviewed him on February 20, 1984, at her home in San Francisco. It was the first time in 11 years that Spielberg had been interviewed for a job.

Although *The Color Purple* received 11 Academy Award nominations, not a single Oscar was awarded to the film. Spielberg was nominated as one of the producers, but he was conspicuously left out of the Best Director category. Spielberg did receive his first Directors Guild of America Award for *The Color Purple*.

Samuel Spielberg. On November 27, 1985, when
Max was five months old, Steven Spielberg and Amy
Irving were married in a private ceremony at the
courthouse in Santa Fe, New Mexico. ⌐

E.T. *gave Spielberg the opportunity to work with a young leading cast.*

Spielberg with his wife, Kate Capshaw, at the seventy-ninth Academy Awards in 2007

FROM SHAME TO HONOR

hree-and-a-half years passed while Spielberg and Irving continued making movies. Yet their busy schedules took a toll on their marriage. In 1989, the two divorced. Spielberg reportedly paid Irving a divorce settlement of

$100 million, half of his fortune at the time and one of the most costly celebrity divorces to date.

The following year, Spielberg renewed his friendship with Kate Capshaw, the leading actress in *Indiana Jones and the Temple of Doom*. Their relationship blossomed into romance, and on October 12, 1991, Spielberg and Capshaw married.

Spielberg was still directing and producing. His 1989 film, *Indiana Jones and the Last Crusade*, was a huge success, but several films that followed were disappointing. *Empire of the Sun*, a film about a British boy separated from his parents in Shanghai during World War II, had been praised by critics but did not do well at the box office. *Always*, a film about a modern-day daredevil pilot who fights forest fires, had mixed reviews and was only moderately successful. Reviewers and audiences were critical of *Hook*, the story of a middle-aged Peter Pan

Kate Capshaw

Kate Capshaw began her acting career in the soap opera *The Edge of Night*. She was one of 120 actresses who vied for the part of Willie Scott in Spielberg's film *Indiana Jones and the Temple of Doom*. Capshaw got the part. Although raised as an Episcopalian, Capshaw converted to Judaism before marrying Steven Spielberg in 1991. Her interest in Judaism inspired Spielberg to return to his Jewish roots, follow more Jewish teachings and traditions, and raise his children in the Jewish faith.

played by Robin Williams. Spielberg expected *Hook* to be his last big film, but he was wrong. He turned his attention to something bigger and greater. By 1993, he would reach a new height of success, directing two blockbusters—*Jurassic Park* and *Schindler's List*. One would be the highest-grossing film of its time, and they would both sweep the Oscars.

Dinosaurs Come to Life

The concept for *Jurassic Park* began in 1989 when Spielberg met with author Michael Crichton to discuss his new book about an amusement park filled with cloned dinosaurs. That night, Spielberg read the novel; the next day he asked Crichton for film rights. The following year, Crichton finally chose Spielberg to direct the film.

It was not until August 1992 that Spielberg began the enormous $95 million project of *Jurassic*

Giving Back

In 1990, Spielberg and Peter Samuelson founded Starbright, an organization dedicated to helping kids cope with their illnesses through technology-based computer programs. The programs entertain, educate, and help kids connect with others in similar circumstances. In 2004, Starbright merged with the Starlight Foundation forming what is known today as Starlight Starbright Children's Foundation.

Spielberg on the set of Jurassic Park *with two of the film's actors*

Park in Hawaii. Two years had been spent in preproduction—writing the script, making robotic dinosaurs, creating special effects. By November, Spielberg had finished filming, and the project went into the editing stages. John Williams finished composing the score, and George Lucas and his crew from Industrial Light & Magic added the special effects. *Jurassic Park* premiered on June 9, 1993, bringing in $47 million its first weekend. It eventually grossed $357 million in the United States.

A Project Close to the Heart

As soon as Spielberg finished filming *Jurassic Park*, he flew to Poland to begin work on *Schindler's List*. At once, Spielberg was absorbed in directing. This was the story that had gripped his heart and returned him to his Jewish roots—the past he had been so ashamed of when he was growing up. When Spielberg began filming *Schindler's List*, he admitted,

[I was] hit in the face with my personal life. My upbringing. My Jewishness. The stories my grandparents told me about the Shoah. And Jewish life came pouring back into my heart. I cried all the time.[1]

Schindler's Story

Schindler's List begins in 1939, just after the start of World War II, when the German Nazis force Polish Jews in the area to relocate to a ghetto in Kráków, Poland. The Nazis soon cleared out the ghetto, transporting the Jews to concentration camps outside the city while killing protestors, the elderly, and the ill.

The film tells the story of Oskar Schindler, a businessman who bribed Germans so he could hire Jews to work in his factory. He made a list with the names of the Jews he wanted to hire and then presented it to the German commander. For the people on his list, it was the difference between life and death. Schindler spent most of his fortune paying off Germans so they would release more Jews on his list. He protected his workers from the Nazi guards assigned to his factory and allowed them to observe the traditions of their faith.

When the Russian army liberated the city, the factory workers presented him with a ring made from gold fillings they had extracted from their teeth and melted. Engraved on it were the words, "He who saves the life of one man saves the world entire."

He called the film his "journey from shame to honor."[2]

Spielberg knew he would not be able to handle the emotional experience of this journey without his family. He and Capshaw now had five children—Max, Jessica, Theo, Sasha, and Sawyer. They all stayed in Poland during the filming of *Schindler's List*. Spielberg also brought his parents and his rabbi. When his mother's second husband became too ill to travel, Spielberg made arrangements for his entire medical team to make the trip with him.

AUTHENTICITY

Spielberg wanted to make *Schindler's List* as authentic as possible. *Schindler's List* was filmed on location, where the Holocaust took place. Spielberg shot scenes at the Jewish ghetto in Warsaw. He wanted to film the Auschwitz scenes at the real sites, but the World Jewish Congress refused to let him

Directing for the Story's Sake

Steven Spielberg would not accept a salary for directing *Schindler's List*. He expected the film to fail and called a salary "blood money." The film premiered in late 1993 in New York, Los Angeles, and Toronto. It grossed $96 million in the United States and more than $321 million worldwide.

Spielberg and his wife pausing near the remains of the Auschwitz concentration camp

film inside the camp. Undaunted, Spielberg had an exact replica constructed right next to Auschwitz. Spielberg also filmed at an abandoned building that had been Schindler's factory. He hired Polish Jews for Schindler's workers and Germans for the parts of Nazis.

Spielberg did not expect *Schindler's List* to do well at the box office. "That's how pessimistic I was that there was a climate ready to accept essentially a movie about racial hatred," Spielberg said.[3] But he was wrong. The film would gross more than $321 million worldwide.

Before the film was released, Spielberg arranged for his mother and her husband to see it alone at a theater. After the showing, Spielberg wanted his mother's reaction, but she was unable to speak. It was an emotional film for many viewers. The sound of sobbing was heard after a screening of the film at the Simon Wiesenthal Center/Museum of Tolerance in Los Angeles.

On March 21, 1994, *Schindler's List* received an Oscar for Best Picture. John Williams won for Best Original Score and Janusz Kaminski for Cinematography. Four more Oscars were awarded that night to *Schindler's*

Holocaust Survivor

Branko Lustig, a producer of *Schindler's List*, was a prisoner at Auschwitz when he was a child. The Nazis killed all his family members except for his mother. Lustig's left arm is tattooed with the number the Nazis branded him with while at Auschwitz. During filming, Lustig shared this and other Holocaust experiences with set and costume designers.

List. At the end of the night, one of them—Best Director—went to Steven Spielberg. It was his first Academy Award for directing, but it would not be his last. ⌐

Spielberg with Liam Neeson during the filming of Schindler's List

Steven Spielberg, third from left, with survivors of the Holocaust at the tenth anniversary of the Shoah Foundation in 2004

DREAMWORKS

teven Spielberg was emotionally and physically exhausted when he finished *Schindler's List*. He took a break from filmmaking, but he certainly was not idle. In 1994, he established Survivors of the Shoah Visual History Foundation to collect recorded testimonies of survivors and witnesses of the Holocaust. Over the next five years, nearly 52,000 interviews were recorded and archived for educational purposes.

Spielberg also helped create the Jurassic Park River Adventure at Universal Studios Hollywood. The attraction features simulated dinosaurs in their natural habitats. When the raptors break loose in the adventure, the only escape from the jaws of Tyrannosaurus rex is a steep drop into complete darkness.

The "Dream Team"

In 1994, Spielberg joined Jeffrey Katzenberg and David Geffen to found DreamWorks SKG (initials of their last names). It was a film, TV, music, and interactive video company. Katzenberg had experience at Walt Disney Studios, where he worked on popular animated features

Jurassic Park, the Ride

The Jurassic Park River Adventure at Universal Studios Hollywood was being built while *Jurassic Park* was still being filmed. The water ride in boats starts at Ultasaur Lagoon, where gentle dinosaurs roam. The boats pass through Stegosaur Springs and head for Hadrosaur Cove. There, an escaped Hadrosaur bursts from the water, striking the boat. At the Velociraptor area of the dinosaur park, where the fences have been torn down, the boats climb a ramp, and two raptors try to attack. The T. rex cage is open, and Spitters attack. As the T. rex charges, the boats plunge down an 85-foot (26-m) drop.

DreamWorks cofounders David Geffen, Steven Spielberg, and Jeffrey Katzenberg, left to right

such as *The Little Mermaid*, *Beauty and the Beast*, *Aladdin*, and *The Lion King*. Geffen's background was in music, an industry that had made him a billionaire. With Spielberg's know-how in filmmaking, the company seemed to have limitless possibilities. The news media dubbed it the "Dream Team."

Capshaw was concerned that DreamWorks would take too much of her husband's time away from his family. In addition to DreamWorks, Spielberg was

still directing and producing movies and running the
Shoah Foundation. But Spielberg promised to make
time for his family. "All important things get done
in my life," he said. "Somehow this [DreamWorks]
is all fitting nicely into my life and I'm still home
by six and I'm still home on weekends. That's the
miracle."[1]

FILMING AND FUN

When Spielberg started directing movies again in
1997, he turned to something fun—a sequel to *Jurassic
Park*. The news came as a surprise since Spielberg
did not often film sequels. He regularly received
thousands of letters, many of them from children,
requesting sequels to his most popular films. He had
tried several *Jaws* sequels, but he was not pleased with
the results. His attempts had taught him to preserve
the quality of movies by allowing them to stand
alone. He especially wanted to protect *E.T. the Extra-
Terrestrial*. Spielberg said,

> *I didn't want to do anything that would blemish its memory
> with a sequel that would not be—could not possibly be—its
> superior. . . . I didn't want to mess with something that I
> thought was almost a perfect little movie.*[2]

He did not feel that way about *Jurassic Park*, however. In fact, he placed it in the bottom five of his movies. He named his sequel *The Lost World Jurassic Park*. In the film, dinosaurs take over an island where a team of scientists is studying dinosaurs in their native habitat. Another group of people on the island are trying to capture the dinosaurs and take them to a second Jurassic Park in San Diego.

The Lost World Jurassic Park, released in 1997, broke box-office records with sales of $72 million the first weekend. It was the biggest opening weekend of its time. It held on to that record for four-and-a-half years, until *Harry Potter and the Sorcerer's Stone* outsold it in November 2001. It also passed the $100 million mark in six days, which was faster than any other film at that time. Critics such as Roger Ebert praised the dinosaurs and special effects but claimed that Spielberg made the movie only because he was pressured into a sequel.

DreamWorks' Hits and Misses

Over the years, DreamWorks produced some of the top animated feature films in the industry. DreamWorks Animation was responsible for the Oscar-winning *Shrek*, as well as *Shrek 2*, *Shark Tale*,

Madagascar, *Over the Hedge*, *Shrek the Third*, *Bee Movie*, and *Kung Fu Panda*. DreamWorks Pictures laid claim to Academy Award-winning films such as *Gladiator*, *American Beauty*, and *A Beautiful Mind*.

But not all DreamWorks movies won awards or became blockbusters. The 1997 antislavery film *Amistad*, directed by Steven Spielberg, did not do well at the box office. Spielberg had once again turned to a serious theme based on a historic event—the 1839 rebellion on the *Amistad*, a Spanish slave ship. On the high seas off the coast of Cuba, 53 African slaves had revolted against their captors, killing all but the two men who promised to take them back to Africa. Instead, the men handed them over to the U.S. Navy. The Africans ended up in U.S. court, fighting for their freedom.

Like *Schindler's List*, the film was an emotional reenactment of

Among the Best

In June 2008, the American Film Institute revealed its "Ten Top Ten"—the best ten films in ten American film genres. More than 1,500 people from the industry were polled. Spielberg's films were among the chosen: *E.T. the Extraterrestrial* was number three in the sci-fi film category. In the epic films category, *Schindler's List* was number three and *Saving Private Ryan* was number eight.

an agonizing historical event. The cast and crew sometimes wept over the moving reality of the scenes. Spielberg later said,

> *While I was making this film, I never felt I was telling someone else's story. I felt like I was telling everyone's story. This is a story that people of all nationalities and races should know.* [3]

Spielberg also made the film for his two adopted African-American children. Roger Ebert described *Schindler's List* and *Amistad* as "ways good men try to work realistically within an evil system to spare a few of its victims." [4]

Saving Private Ryan

In 1998, DreamWorks produced and Spielberg directed another historical film—*Saving Private Ryan*. The World War II film, set during the 1944 invasion of Normandy, France, was a success with the critics as well as the public, and it became the highest-grossing film of the year.

To make the film, Spielberg again teamed up with some of the people who had made his past achievements possible—John Williams for music, Janusz Kaminski for cinematography, and Michael Kahn for editing. He cast Tom Hanks as U.S. Army

Spielberg directing cast members of Saving Private Ryan

Captain John H. Miller, who, with a small band of soldiers, searches for paratrooper Private First Class James Francis Ryan (played by Matt Damon). Ryan's three brothers had been killed in the war, all within days of each other. In order to save their mother the grief of possibly losing her last son, an army general orders that Ryan be found and brought home alive.

The realistic opening scene that reenacts D-day on
June 6, 1944, at Omaha Beach in France thrust
the film to the top of the charts. Critics called it a
masterpiece.

Because Omaha Beach was a protected historical
landmark, the opening scene of *Saving Private Ryan*
was filmed in Ireland. The beach had remarkable
similarities to Omaha Beach. For the battle scenes on
land, a country village in England was transformed
into a replica of a French village. Since there were
not enough authentic uniforms from World War
II available, Spielberg's costume crew made 3,000
uniforms. The soldiers also needed boots. The
company that had manufactured the original World
War II boots for U.S. soldiers still had the original
pattern and made 2,000 pairs for the film. The
brand new uniforms and boots then went through a
process to make them appear battle worn.

Spielberg wanted the film to look like a newsreel,
a documentary. So he used handheld cameras, a
technique he had used in *Schindler's List*, *E.T.*, and
other films. There were no cranes or booms;
Spielberg wanted the audience to feel like they were
there, part of the action on the beach or in the
village.

Saving Private Ryan received rave reviews. One reviewer said,

> *Perhaps realizing that there was no avoiding the old truism that war is hell, Spielberg decided to underline, italicize and boldface it in startling terms that no one could miss. No further commentary is needed when the raw brutality of combat is presented as indelibly as it is here.*[5]

Several critics' associations such as New York Critics Circle and the Los Angeles Film Critics Association named *Saving Private Ryan* Film of the Year. It also won the Golden Globe Award for Best Picture (Drama), and Spielberg received a Golden

Boot Camp

To prepare the actors for the battle scenes in *Saving Private Ryan*, Spielberg hired U.S. Marine Captain Dale Dye to put them through a ten-day boot camp. Dye, a wounded Vietnam veteran, got the men up at five in the morning, fed them rations, and made them hike through all types of terrain, in good weather and in bad. When the men complained, Dye shouted, "You're embodying the souls of the fallen comrades who made the world safe for democracy. So you're not going to do that lightly. You're going to know the weaponry, you're going to know the tactics, you're going to know the background, and you're going to know the history."[6]

Some of the actors were hesitant to undergo the boot camp experience. But after the ten days were over, there was a real bond between the men. Tom Hanks believed the experience gave them more understanding of their roles. He said, "We were playing soldiers who were tired and miserable and wanted to go home, and I don't think we could have done that justice without having experienced what Dale Dye put us through."[7]

Globe for Best Director. At the Academy Awards, *Saving Private Ryan* received 11 nominations and was awarded five Oscars, including the Best Director award for Spielberg.

The Directors Guild of America and the Producers Guild of America also recognized Spielberg that year, presenting him with the Darryl F. Zanuck Award for Theatrical Motion Picture Producer of the Year. The guild also awarded Spielberg the prestigious Milestone Award for his historic contribution to the motion picture industry. Spielberg's rise to the top, however, would not stop him from continuing to dream and create.

Spielberg with his Golden Globes for Saving Private Ryan

In 2009, Spielberg was honored with the Cecil B. DeMille Award at the sixty-sixth Golden Globe Awards.

DREAMING FOR A LIVING

In a 1985 interview with *Time* magazine, Spielberg said,

I dream for a living. Once a month the sky falls on my head, I come to, and I see another movie I want to make. . . . My problem is that my imagination won't turn off. I wake up so excited I can't eat breakfast. I've never run out of energy.[1]

Indeed, Spielberg has never grown tired of filmmaking. It energizes him; it is who he is. In 2001, 54-year-old Spielberg returned to science fiction and directed *A.I. Artificial Intelligence*. He again teamed up with John Williams, Janusz Kaminski, and Michael Kahn. He also returned to working with a child actor, Haley Joel Osment, who played the part of David, an android, or a humanlike robot programmed with the ability to love.

Other movies hit the box office, including *Minority Report*, which connected Spielberg and Tom Cruise in a science-fiction style mystery. In 2002, Spielberg's *Catch Me If You Can* again molded his childhood into a film. He related to the lead character, Frank Abagnale (played by Leonardo DiCaprio), who was raised

Video Games

For much of his life Spielberg enjoyed playing video games. Eventually, he became involved in creating scenarios for adventure games such as *The Dig*. In 2005, Spielberg signed with Electronic Arts to work together on three games and a puzzle game for the Wii. He created the World War II shooting game *Medal of Honor* series in which the player fights for the United States.

Director versus Producer

Film directors and producers have very different roles in making a movie. Directors visualize the scenes and oversee the artistic and dramatic aspects of a film. Directors control the tone of the film, the camera angles, the lighting, and the set designs. They tell the actors how to play their characters, and they shape the story. After the film has been shot, the director supervises the editing process, controlling the close-ups, the coloring, and the music. Film producers manage the financial and physical aspects of the film. They control the conditions under which the film is shot.

in suburbia and became devastated by his parents' divorce. Abagnale was much like Spielberg with his amazing mind and his ability to succeed at whatever he tried, all at a very young age. That year Spielberg also produced *Men in Black II*. In 2004, he directed and produced *The Terminal* starring Tom Hanks, who had become one of Spielberg's closest friends.

In 2005, Spielberg teamed up with Tom Cruise and Dakota Fanning for a remake of the 1953 movie *War of the Worlds*. Spielberg believed it was time for a remake because the world had changed—the United States had been attacked by terrorists on September 11, 2001. The science-fiction film that featured violent aliens had noticeable references to September 11. A *Los Angeles Times* film critic described some of the scenes: "Terrified residents rush through the streets covered in ash and dust;

Spielberg, right, visualizing a scene in Minority Report

handmade missing-person posters line the sidewalks; commercial airliners fall from the sky."[2] The film was a huge success, grossing nearly $600 million.

MORE AWARDS

In 2005, Spielberg again returned to his Jewish heritage to make a film. It was called *Munich*, the story of 11 Israeli athletes at the 1972 Olympics in Munich, Germany. Spielberg had watched the horrifying events unfold on television when the Palestinian terrorist group Black September kidnapped the athletes and executed them one by one. *Munich* went further with the story, a part that could not be confirmed. It told of five Israelis who pursued and killed the terrorists, a plan called the "Wrath of God" under the direction of Israeli Prime Minister Golda Meir.

Reviews for *Munich* were mixed and several marked it as a controversial film. Some called it "spectacularly gripping and unsettling . . . grave and haunted."[3] Others reported that Israelis were refusing to see it. *Munich* was nominated for five Academy Awards but did not win any. Spielberg received Best Director from the Directors Guild of America, the Golden Globe Awards, and the Online Film Critics Society, as well as the Critics' Choice Award for Best Director. John Williams and Michael Kahn also received awards for music and editing.

Writing *Munich*

Spielberg turned down three screenplays for *Munich* before he read the one he wanted to make into a movie. It was written by Pulitzer Prize-winning screenwriter and playwright Tony Kushner. Kushner explained his goals and challenges in writing the screenplay: "I never like to draw lessons for people. It's not an essay; it's art. But I think I can safely say the conflict between national security and ethics raised deep questions in terms of working on the film. I was surprised to discover how much the story had to do with nationality versus family, and questions about home and being in conflict with somebody else over a territory that seems home to both people."[4]

In 2005, Spielberg also produced *The Legend of Zorro*, *Memoirs of a Geisha*, and the TV miniseries *Into the West*. It was also the year Spielberg, Katzenberg, and Geffen sold DreamWorks SKG to Paramount Pictures for $1.6 billion. They kept DreamWorks Animation SKG. For the first time in more than a decade, Spielberg directed a film that did not have the DreamWorks label. In May 2008, *Indiana Jones and the Kingdom of the Crystal Skull* was released, again starring Harrison Ford. Spielberg called Karen Allen, who played the role of Marion Ravenwood in *Raiders of the Lost Ark*, and told her he wanted her in the fourth Indiana Jones adventure film that some called *Indy 4*. It received good reviews and did well at the box office, but some moviegoers were disappointed by the introduction of aliens, a theme uncharacteristic of the first three films.

TV Miniseries

Spielberg has worked on several TV miniseries throughout his career. A TV miniseries is a story that is told over a set number of television episodes. In addition to directing *Into the West*, Spielberg was a producer for *Band of Brothers*, which appeared on HBO in 2001, and for *Taken*, which appeared on the Sci Fi Channel in 2002.

Continuing to Dream

Spielberg is not finished yet with his dreams or his goals—and he may never stop seeing the world through the lens of a camera. He continues to dream and create and entertain, something he seems driven to do. Again and again, he returns to filmmaking and a handful of themes that never seem to tire viewers. People relate to his stories and to his characters—ordinary people who come in contact with the extraordinary.

Spielberg also shares part of himself and bits of his past in his films. Audiences can relate to Spielberg's deep pain from divorce, the loneliness of growing up differently, the anguish of vile wars, and a fascination with the sky and the unknown. And nearly everyone enjoys his wide-eyed wonder of childhood—in the magical way that Spielberg sees it.

Reality TV

In 2006, Spielberg teamed up with reality TV expert Mark Burnett to create *On the Lot,* an ill-fated series about aspiring amateur filmmakers who compete for a $1 million deal with DreamWorks. The failure of the show was blamed on several things—even if someone was a big winner, the viewers might never see that person again; the judges were uninteresting; and in the end, the audience did not care enough. The one-page *On the Lot* Web site congratulates the winner, Will Bigham, and thanks the other talented film-makers. It ends with the words, "That's a Wrap!"

He also has recreated and brought reality to history—a history often rooted in his own past and a history that defines who he is. With accuracy and passion, he has transported moviegoers to the world's grizzliest death camps and to gruesome battle scenes. These are not intended to entertain, but to make an indelible mark on people.

Steven Spielberg has made his impact on the world as one of the most influential directors of all time. He has provided moviegoers with

Spielberg and the Beijing Olympics

In 2006, Steven Spielberg was named artistic adviser for the opening and closing ceremonies of the 2008 Beijing Olympics in China. He was slated to work with Zhang Yimou, a celebrated Chinese filmmaker and chief director for the Olympic ceremonies. Spielberg said, "It's a great honor to accept this appointment as an overseas adviser." He added,

Our one goal is to give the world a taste of peace, friendship, cooperation and understanding. Through the visual and performing arts, the art of music, the art of dance and the art of celebration of life, all of us are dedicated to making these Olympic opening and closing ceremonies the most emotional everyone has ever seen.[5]

In February 2008, Spielberg withdrew as artistic adviser. For a year, he had tried unsuccessfully to convince China's President Hu Jintao to do more to end Sudan's attacks in the region of Darfur, Africa. Hundreds of thousands of people had died from government attacks, starvation, and disease. Spielberg said, "I find that my conscience will not allow me to continue business as usual." He added,

At this point, my time and energy must be spent not on Olympic ceremonies, but on doing all I can to help bring an end to the unspeakable crimes against humanity that continue to be committed in Darfur.[6]

a breathtaking escape into the world of captivating entertainment. He also has offered audiences a new outlook on life and a deeper sense of who they are. Spielberg has touched lives, much like E.T. touched Elliot with his glowing, energized finger and made him see himself and the world in a different way. ⌒

Year Awarded	Honor/Award
1987	Irving G. Thalberg Memorial Award
1989	Distinguished Eagle Scout Award
1994	Oscar, Best Director, *Schindler's List* (1993)
1994	Oscar, Best Picture, *Schindler's List* (1993)
1994	Golden Globe, Best Director, *Schindler's List* (1993)
1995	Lifetime Achievement Award from the American Film Institute
1998	Named one of the "100 Most Important People of the Century" by *Time* magazine
1999	Oscar, Best Director, *Saving Private Ryan* (1998)
1999	Golden Globe, Best Director, *Saving Private Ryan* (1998)
1999	Department of Defense Medal for Distinguished Public Service
2000	Lifetime Achievement Award from the Directors Guild of America
2001	Honorary Knight Commander of the Order of the British Empire
2005	Named one of "35 Who Made a Difference" by *Smithsonian* magazine
2006	Gold Hugo Lifetime Achievement Award
2009	Cecil B. DeMille Award

Steven Spielberg has received numerous awards and honors.

TIMELINE

1946

Steven Allan Spielberg is born on December 18 in Cincinnati, Ohio.

1952

Spielberg sees his first movie, *The Greatest Show on Earth*, at age five.

1958

Spielberg films *The Last Gunfight* to earn his Eagle Scout badge.

1965

Spielberg enrolls at California State University, Long Beach and works three days a week at Universal Studios.

1968

Spielberg films *Amblin'* and lands a seven-year contract with Universal Studios.

1971

Spielberg's *Duel* airs as the ABC Movie of the Weekend and receives rave reviews.

1960

Spielberg films *Fighter Squad*, a 15-minute, black-and-white World War II movie.

1962

Escape to Nowhere, Spielberg's first scripted movie, wins first prize at the Canyon Films Junior Film Festival.

1964

Spielberg's first feature film, *Firelight*, premieres at the Phoenix Little Theatre.

1975

Jaws breaks all previous box-office records.

1978

Spielberg receives his first Academy Award nomination for Best Director for *Close Encounters of the Third Kind*.

1982

Spielberg receives his second Best Director Academy Award nomination for *Raiders of the Lost Ark*.

TIMELINE

1983

Spielberg receives his third Academy Award nomination for Best Director for *E.T. the Extra-Terrestrial.*

1984

Spielberg cofounds Amblin Entertainment.

1985

Spielberg marries Amy Irving; they divorce in 1989.

1994

Spielberg wins his first Academy Award for Best Director for *Schindler's List.*

1994

Spielberg founds Survivors of the Shoah Visual History Foundation.

1994

Spielberg forms DreamWorks SKG with Jeffrey Katzenberg and David Geffen.

1990	1991	1993
Spielberg cofounds Starbright, an organization that helps children with illnesses.	Spielberg marries Kate Capshaw.	Spielberg directs *Jurassic Park* and *Schindler's List*.

1999	2006	2009
Saving Private Ryan receives five Academy Awards, and Spielberg receives his second Academy Award for Best Director.	Named artistic adviser for the opening and closing ceremonies of the 2008 Olympics, Spielberg later withdraws over political issues.	Spielberg receives the Cecil B. DeMille Award for outstanding contributions to the entertainment industry.

Essential Facts

Date of Birth

December 18, 1946

Place of Birth

Cincinnati, Ohio

Parents

Arnold Spielberg and Leah (Posner) Adler

Education

Arcadia High School, Phoenix, Arizona; Saratoga High School, Saratoga, California; California State University, Long Beach (received a BA in 2002)

Marriages

❖ Amy Irving (1985–1989)
❖ Kate Capshaw (1991)

Children

❖ With Irving: Max
❖ With Capshaw: Jessica (daughter from Capshaw's previous marriage to Robert Capshaw), Theo (son adopted by Capshaw before her marriage to Steven; Steven later adopted Theo), Sasha, Sawyer, Mikaela, and Destry

CAREER HIGHLIGHTS

Spielberg has won two Academy Awards for Best Director. He won for *Schindler's List* in 1994 and for *Saving Private Ryan* in 1998.

SOCIETAL CONTRIBUTION

❖ Spielberg has directed films that have captured the hearts and minds of hundreds of thousands of viewers. Several of his films, including *Schindler's List*, *Amistad*, and *Saving Private Ryan*, have brought historic events to the screen.

❖ In 1991, Spielberg cofounded Starbright, an organization that helps children with illnesses.

❖ In 1994, Spielberg established the Survivors of the Shoah Visual History Foundation to record survivors' and witnesses' testimonies of the Holocaust.

CONFLICTS

❖ Spielberg struggled with his Jewish heritage throughout his youth and adulthood. He came to terms with his faith after filming *Schindler's List*.

❖ Some people have criticized Spielberg's films for being too mainstream and entertaining, rather than artistic and thought-provoking.

QUOTE

"Steven Spielberg is as close to a natural-born cameraman as anybody I've ever known of. . . . As far as I'm concerned he's the most gifted person in motion pictures. Not just today—ever."
—*Chuck Silvers, head of Universal Studios editorial department, 1968*

ADDITIONAL RESOURCES

SELECT BIBLIOGRAPHY

Corliss, Richard. "I Dream for a Living." *Time*. 15 July 1985. 6 Sept. 2008 <http://www.time.com/time/magazine/article/0,9171,959634-2,00.html>.

Friedman, Lester D., and Brent Notbohm, eds. *Steven Spielberg Interviews*. Jackson, MS: University Press of Mississippi, 2000.

Jackson, Kathi. *Steven Spielberg: A Biography*. Westport, CT: Greenwood Press, 2007.

Kakutani, Michiko. "The Two Faces of Spielberg—Horror vs. Hope." *New York Times*. 30 May 1982.

McBride, Joseph. *Steven Spielberg: A Biography*. New York: Simon & Schuster, 1997.

FURTHER READING

Gish, Melissa. *Steven Spielberg*. Mankato, MN: Creative Education, 2000.

Rubin, Susan Goldman. *Steven Spielberg: Crazy for Movies*. New York: Harry N. Abrams, Inc., 2001.

Woog, Adam. *Steven Spielberg*. San Diego, CA: Lucent Books, 1999.

Web Links

To learn more about Steven Spielberg, visit ABDO Publishing Company online at **www.abdopublishing.com**. Web sites about Steven Spielberg are featured on our Book Links page. These links are routinely monitored and updated to provide the most current information available.

Places to Visit

United States Holocaust Memorial Museum
100 Raoul Wallenberg Place Southwest
Washington DC 20024-2126
202-488-0400
www.ushmm.org
The museum displays items and information about the Holocaust through exhibits and films.

Universal Studios Florida
6000 Universal Boulevard, Orlando, FL 32819
407-363-8000
www.universalorlando.com
The Universal Studios theme park allows a behind-the-scenes tour of a real film and television studio, including live performances and live broadcasts.

Universal Studios Hollywood
70 Universal City Plaza, Universal City, CA 91608
818-622-3801
www.universalstudioshollywood.com
This movie-based theme park also includes a behind-the-scenes studio tour of some of the most famous television and movie sets of all time, including Steven Spielberg films such as *War of the Worlds*.

GLOSSARY

Academy Awards
Annual awards presented by the Academy of Motion Picture Arts and Sciences to honor professionals in the film industry.

cinematography
The technique of photographing movies, including the shooting and the development of the film.

concentration camp
A place where groups of people are detained, often during a time of war.

director
The person responsible for what a film looks like on the screen. The director is also in charge of sets, camera placement, acting, lighting, and other things that give a film its look and tone.

draft
A system that automatically recruits individuals into military service.

feature
A motion picture made for showing in a movie theater as the main attraction, usually running 40 minutes or longer.

film editor
A person who connects film sequences together to form an entire movie.

footage
A portion of filmed material.

Holocaust
The systematic extermination of 6 million Jews and other "undesirables" by Nazi Germany during World War II, a plan that Adolf Hitler called the "Final Solution of the Jewish Question."

paranormal
>Something that cannot be explained scientifically.

producer
>The person who oversees the physical production of a film, such as staff hiring, finding financial backers, and arranging for film distribution.

score
>A musical composition.

screening
>The first presentation of a motion picture.

screenwriter
>A person who writes movie scripts, which include descriptions of scenes and sometimes camera directions.

set
>The scenery for a film, television, or theater production.

short
>A short film that typically runs between 20 and 40 minutes in length.

stop motion
>An automatic device for stopping the motion of a movie camera so objects can be moved by small amounts between individually filmed frames, creating the illusion of movement when the frames are played in a continuous succession.

storyboard
>A series of drawings that illustrates the visual sequence of a film.

Source Notes

Chapter 1. An Oscar at Last
1. "Steven Spielberg Winning an Oscar for 'Schindler's List.'" *You Tube*. 6 Aug. 2008 <http://www.youtube.com/watch?v=7bRNEZVNVSs>.
2. Ibid.
3. Ibid.
4. Lester D. Friedman and Brent Notbohm, eds. *Steven Spielberg Interviews*. Jackson, MS: University Press of Mississippi, 2000. 159.
5. Lester D. Friedman. *Citizen Spielberg*. Urbana/Chicago: University of Illinois Press, 2006. 303.

Chapter 2. Growing Up Jewish
1. Joseph McBride. *Steven Spielberg: A Biography*. New York: Simon & Schuster, 1997. 33–34.
2. Ibid. 42.
3. Emily Soares. Rev. of *Hook*, dir. Steven Spielberg. *Turner Classic Movies Online*. 27 Feb. 2009 <http://www.tcm.com/thismonth/article.jsp?cid=188900&mainArticleId=188898>.
4. Joseph McBride. *Steven Spielberg: A Biography*. New York: Simon & Schuster, 1997. 52.

Chapter 3. Boy with a Camera
1. Michiko Kakutani. "The Two Faces of Spielberg—Horror vs. Hope." *New York Times Online*. 30 May 1982. 9 Oct. 2008 <http://movies.nytimes.com/movie/review?res=9805E7DE1038F933A05756C0A964948260>.
2. Joseph McBride. *Steven Spielberg: A Biography*. New York: Simon & Schuster, 1997. 246.
3. Lester D. Friedman and Brent Notbohm, eds. *Steven Spielberg Interviews*. Jackson, MS: University Press of Mississippi, 2000. 187.
4. Joseph McBride. *Steven Spielberg: A Biography*. New York: Simon & Schuster, 1997. 83.

5. Lester D. Friedman and Brent Notbohm, eds. *Steven Spielberg Interviews*. Jackson, MS: University Press of Mississippi, 2000. 187.
6. Richard Corliss and Marth Smilgis. "Steve's Summer Magic." *Time Online*. 31 May 1982. 9 Oct. 2008 < http://www.time.com/time/magazine/article/0,9171,925427-10,00.html>.
7. Joseph McBride. *Steven Spielberg: A Biography*. New York: Simon & Schuster, 1997. 99.
8. Ibid. 108.

Chapter 4. A Foot in the Door
1. Bernard Weinraub. "Steven Spielberg Faces the Holocaust." *New York Times*. 12 Dec. 1993. 9 Oct. 2008 <http://query.nytimes.com/gst/fullpage.html?res=9F0CE6DD1630F931A25751C1A9659 58260&sec=&spon=&pagewanted=4>.
2. Andrew Gordon. *Empire of Dreams: The Science Fiction and Fantasy Films of Steven Spielberg*. Lanham, MD: Rowman & Littlefield Publishers, 2007. 99.
3. Joseph McBride. *Steven Spielberg: A Biography*. New York: Simon & Schuster, 1997. 110.
4. Ibid. 162–163.

Chapter 5. World of Film
1. Joseph McBride. *Steven Spielberg: A Biography*. New York: Simon & Schuster, 1997. 198.
2. Ibid. 241.
3. Ibid. 52.
4. Ibid. 272.
5. Frank Rich. "The Aliens Are Coming!" *Time Online*. 7 Nov. 1977. 5 Sep. 2008 <http://www.time.com/time/magazine/article/0,9171,947980-4,00.html>.

Source Notes Continued

Chapter 6. Films and Family

1. Joseph McBride. *Steven Spielberg: A Biography*. New York: Simon & Schuster, 1997. 315.
2. Vincent Canby. "Raiders of the Lost Ark." *New York Times Online*. 12 June 1981. 5 Sept. 2008 <http://movies.nytimes.com/movie/review?res=EE05E7DF173AA42CA1494CC6B6799D836896>.
3. Joseph McBride. *Steven Spielberg: A Biography*. New York: Simon & Schuster, 1997. 323.
4. Lester D. Friedman and Brent Notbohm, eds. *Steven Spielberg Interviews*. Jackson, MS: University Press of Mississippi, 2000. 110.
5. *E.T. the Extra-Terrestrial: The 20th Anniversary Celebration*. Dir. Steven Spielberg. 1982. DVD. Universal, 2002.
6. Joseph McBride. *Steven Spielberg: A Biography*. New York: Simon & Schuster, 1997. 327–328.
7. Ibid. 333.
8. Richard Corliss. "I Dream for a Living." *Time*. 15 July 1985. 6 Sept. 2008 <http://www.time.com/time/magazine/article/0,9171,959634-2,00.html>.

Chapter 7. From Shame to Honor

1. Joseph McBride. *Steven Spielberg: A Biography*. New York: Simon & Schuster, 1997. 414.
2. Ibid.
3. Ibid. 416.

Chapter 8. DreamWorks

1. Joseph McBride. *Steven Spielberg: A Biography*. New York: Simon & Schuster, 1997. 447.
2. Lester D. Friedman and Brent Notbohm, eds. *Steven Spielberg Interviews*. Jackson, MS: University Press of Mississippi, 2000. 197.
3. Trevor B. McCrisken and Andrew Pepper. *American History and Contemporary Hollywood Film: From 1492 to Three Kings*. Edinburgh, Scot.: Edinburgh University Press, 2005. 60.

4. Roger Ebert. Rev. of *Amistad*, dir. Steven Spielberg. 12 Dec. 1997. 10 Sept. 2008 <http://rogerebert.suntimes.com/apps/pbcs. dll/article?AID=/19971212/REVIEWS/712120301/1023>.
5. Todd McCarthy. Rev. of *Saving Private Ryan*, dir. Steven Spielberg. *Variety Online*. 20 July 1998. 10 Sept. 2008 <http://www.variety.com/review/VE1117477699.html?categoryid=31&cs=1&p=0>.
6. Kathi Jackson. *Steven Spielberg: A Biography*. Westport, CT: Greenwood Press, 2007. 71.
7. Behind the Scenes of *Saving Private Ryan*. "Boot Camp." 3 Nov. 2008 <http://rzm.com/pvt.ryan/production/scenes/bootcamp. html>.

Chapter 9. Dreaming for a Living
1. Richard Corliss. "I Dream for a Living." *Time Online*. 15 July 1985. 10 Sept. 2008 <http://www.time.com/time/magazine/article/0,9171,959634-2,00.html>.
2. Carina Chocano. "To Think Like the Masters." *Los Angeles Times Online*. 10 July 2005. 11 Sept. 2008 <http://articles.latimes. com/2005/jul/10/entertainment/ca-spielberg10>.
3. Owen Gleiberman. "Munich (2005). *Entertainment Weekly*. 14 Dec 2005. 11 Sept. 2008 <http://www.ew.com/ew/article/0,,1140761,00.html>.
4. Richard Schickel. "Spielberg Takes On Terror." *Time Online*. 4 Dec. 2005. 13 Jan. 2009 <http://www.time.com/time/magazine/article/0,9171,1137679-1,00.html>.
5. "Big Names Cast in Beijing Olympics Ceremonies' Roles." *China View Online*. 17 Apr. 2006. 14 Sept. 2008 <http://news.xinhuanet. com/english/2006-04/17/content_4433907.htm>.
6. "Spielberg in Darfur Snub to China." *BBC News Online*. 13 Feb. 2008. 11 Sept. 2008 <http://news.bbc.co.uk/2/hi/asia-pacific/7242016.stm>.

INDEX

ABOUT THE AUTHOR

Sue Vander Hook has been writing books for children and young adults for more than 15 years. She especially enjoys writing about historical events and biographies of people who have made a difference in our world. Her published works also include a high school curriculum and series on disease, technology, and sports. Sue lives with her family in Minnesota.

PHOTO CREDITS